PREACHERS AND TEACHERS

PREACHERS AND TEACHERS

NANCY HEVLY

TWENTY–FIRST CENTURY BOOKS

A Division of Henry Holt and Company
New York

Twenty-First Century Books
A Division of Henry Holt and Company, Inc.
115 West 18th Street
New York, NY 10011

Henry Holt ® and colophon are trademarks of
Henry Holt and Company, Inc.
Publishers since 1866

Published in Canada by Fitzhenry & Whiteside Ltd.
195 Allstate Parkway, Markham, Ontario L3R 4T8

Library of Congress Cataloging-in-Publication Data
Hevly, Nancy.

Preachers and teachers / Nancy Hevly. — 1st ed.
p. cm. — (Settling the West)
Includes bibliographical references and index.
1. Clergy—West (U.S.)—History—Juvenile literature. 2. Indians of North America—Missions—West (U.S.)—Juvenile literature. 3. Missionaries—West (U.S.)—Juvenile literature. 4. Teachers—West (U.S.)—History—Juvenile literature. 5. Students—West (U.S.)—Juvenile literature. 6. Frontier and pioneer life—West (U.S.)—Juvenile literature. 7. West (U.S.)—Church History—Juvenile literature. I. Title. II. Series.
BR545.H48 1995
266'.009795—dc20   94–41767
                                                                                  CIP
                                                                                  AC

ISBN 0-8050-2996-6
First Edition 1995

Cover design by Kelly Soong
Interior design by Helene Berinsky

Printed in the United States of America
All first editions are printed on acid-free paper ∞.
10 9 8 7 6 5 4 3 2 1

Photo Credits

pp. 2, 20, 24, 36, 42, 47, 68, 82: North Wind Picture Archives; p. 14: The Bettmann Archive; pp. 16, 17 (both): Arizona Historical Society Library; p. 26: Eastern Washington State Historical Society; p. 39: Oregon Historical Society/OrHi 87846; pp. 40, 62, 72, 75: Washington State Historical Society, Tacoma, Washington; pp. 48, 49: Nevada Historical Society; pp. 52, 63: National Archives; p. 65: Tombstone Courthouse State Historic Park; p. 67: R. K. Smith Collection/U.S. Army Chaplain Museum; p. 77: Courtesy, The Bancroft Library.

EDITOR'S NOTE

A great deal of research went into finding interesting first-person accounts that would give the reader a vivid picture of life on the western frontier. In order to retain the "flavor" of these accounts, original spelling and punctuation have been kept in most instances.

History told in the words of men and women who lived at the time lets us become a part of their lives . . . lives of ordinary people who met extraordinary challenges to settle the West.

—P.C.

CONTENTS

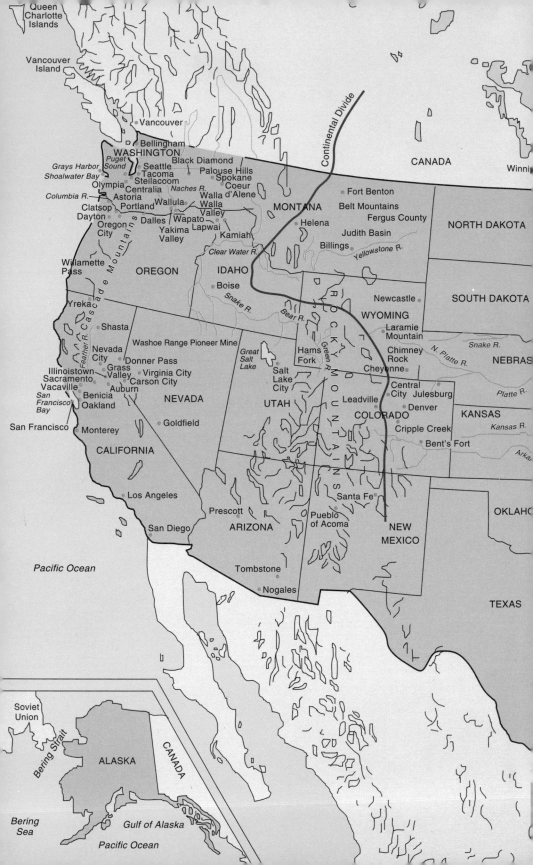

MAJOR TRAILS TO THE WEST

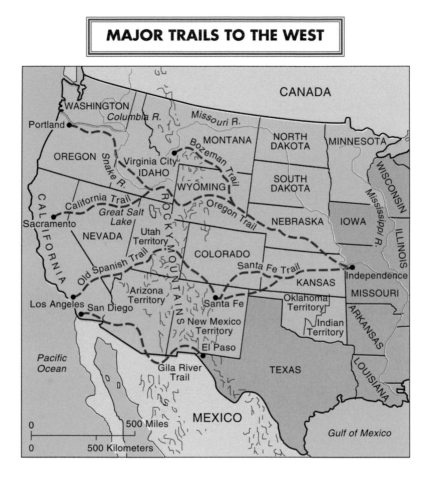

THE PROPHECY

Almost 200 years ago, it is said, an Indian chief of the Spokane people told his young son a strange story.

"When I was a boy there was a night of terror. The sky and the earth shook and rumbled with thunder. In the morning the people saw that everything around them was gray. The trees, the grass, the rocks, their shelters—all were covered by ashes.

"The people were very afraid. They thought it was the end of the world. Then an old man stepped forward, calmed the people and commanded them to hear his message.

"'This is not the end of the world,' the old man said. 'Much more must come to pass before that time arrives. Let me tell you this! A strange people with a skin of a different color, speaking another language and wearing strange clothes will come to us before the world ends. They will bring with them teachers who will show us how to learn things from marks made on leaves bound together in a bundle. Until these people come the world will continue. Let us get to work and clean up these ashes.'"[1]

Scholars say that the chief's account of thunder, the shaking of the earth, and ash falling from the sky was accurate. The "night of terror" took place in 1790, when Mount Saint Helens volcano in the Cascade Range erupted.

The other part of his story also proved to be true. A few years after the chief told his son of the old man's prophecy, preachers and teachers with their books—the "leaves bound together in a bundle"—came to the lands of the Northwest Indians.

1

FOR GOD AND SPAIN

Preachers usually were teachers and teachers often were preachers in the American frontier West. Bibles and book learning traveled together from the time European explorers sailed halfway around the world looking for new lands to claim until settlers carved the wilderness into towns and farms some 300 years later.

In the 1500s Catholic Franciscan missionaries helped explore the Southwest and marched with the Spanish conqueror Francisco Vásquez de Coronado seeking the Seven Cities of Gold. In 1602, when the Spanish navigator Captain Sebastián Vizcaíno sailed up the West Coast of North America, he, like so many who came after him, saw the new land as a place to gain riches and, at the same time, to save souls.

The captain looked upon the welcoming harbors, the towering forests, the clear rivers and lakes. He met the friendly natives who were ignorant of the Christian religion that was as basic to the lives of Europeans as their food and

In the 1500s, Catholic missionaries were a part of Coronado's expedition in the Southwest.

drink. Captain Vizcaíno reported to his ruler and sponsor, the Catholic King Philip III of Spain:

"This land has a genial climate, its waters are good, and it is very fertile. . . . And it is thickly settled with people whom I found to be of gentle disposition . . . and who can be brought readily within the fold of the holy gospel and into subjection to the crown of Your Majesty. . . .

"They manifested great friendship for us and . . . were well affected toward the image of Our Lady [Mary] which I showed to them. . . . They worship different idols . . . and they are well acquainted with silver and gold, and said these were found in the interior. . . .

"From this place the interior can be reached and explored, such exploration promising rich returns . . . and

14

according to the reports I received, there are to be found very numerous peoples akin to those I have referred to—so the door will be opened for the propagation of the faith and the bringing of so many souls to a knowledge of God in order that the seed of the holy gospel may yield a harvest among all these heathen."[1]

Others shared Vizcaíno's vision. To them the new land was a treasure chest waiting to be opened by those who would come to serve their God, to find adventure, to seek their fortunes, and to secure better lives for themselves and their families.

The newcomers would bring their religion with them. As devout Christians, they, like Vizcaíno, could not ignore all those "heathen" ripe for "harvest." They would also bring their schools. Missionaries believed that they must teach as well as preach to the natives. In order to accept the white man's God fully, the Indians—as the newcomers called the natives—must be taught to think, live, and worship as their white brothers and sisters did. The Christians dismissed the natives' own complex religious beliefs, rooted in nature, and their ancient heritage as childish blasphemy.

The link between religion and education prevailed throughout the era of the development of the West. As late as 1875, the United States Board of Indian Commissioners, which supervised the Native American tribes, decreed: "The true policy in dealing with the Indian race, as with every other, for the purpose of elevating them to the social and moral conditions of Christian civilization, consists not so much in feeding or governing the adults as in education of the children."[2]

Almost one hundred years before the American

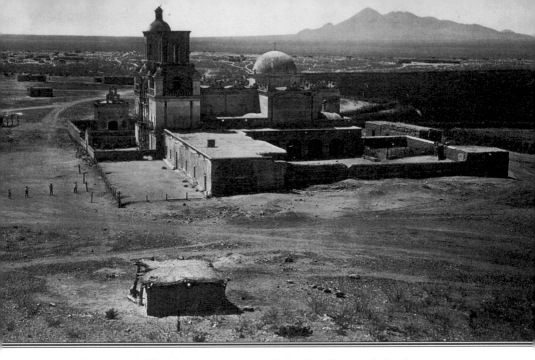

This is the oldest known picture of the San Xavier Mission in Arizona. It was taken around 1881.

colonies declared their independence from Britain and eighty years after Captain Vizcaíno visited the West Coast another Spanish explorer-missionary, Father Eusebio Francisco Kino, was crisscrossing the Southwest. The Catholic church had sent Kino to America in 1681 to take charge of a huge territory that included northern Mexico and southern Arizona.

The humble but energetic Jesuit priest was a long way from his native Tirolean Alps, but he seemed to relish his travels over cactus-covered deserts, rugged mountains, and rushing rivers. He made converts for his church and founded a score of missions that included the first cattle, horse, and sheep ranches in the Southwest. He also imported seeds from Europe and taught the Indians to grow crops.

Because he was a skilled geographer and mapmaker, the missionary priest was named royal cartographer in 1683, and in 1701 he was sent to explore California, which was thought to be an island. Kino traveled around the top of the Gulf of California and made the important discovery that California was not surrounded by water but was part of the mainland.

Father Kino (inset) made this map of the Southwest in 1701.

In one of his reports, Kino described how he met a tribe of Quiquimas Indians and introduced them to horses, as well as to his religion.

"Through the interpreters . . ." he wrote, "we made them some talks on our holy father, which were well received. . . . The natives greatly wondered at many of our things, for they had never seen nor heard of them. They wondered much at the vestment in which mass is said, and at its curious sort of embroidery representing spring. . . . Also it was a matter of much astonishment to them to see our pack animals and mounts, for they had never seen horses or mules or heard of them. And when the Yumas and Pimmas who came with us said to them that our horses could run faster than the most fleet-footed natives, they did not believe it, and it was necessary to put it to the test. Thereupon a cowboy from [our mission] saddled a horse and seven or eight of the most fleet-foot Quiquima runners set out, and although the cowboy at first purposely let them get a little ahead, and they were very gleeful thereat, he afterward left them far behind and very much astonished and amazed."[3]

Father Kino, the "padre on horseback," prepared the way for the Catholic Franciscan priests who arrived in California almost eighty years later.

The church sent Father Junípero Serra to California in 1769 to establish missions to bring the Christian faith to the Indians. At the same time, the Spanish government headquarters in Mexico sent soldiers to secure the new land for Spain and protect the missions, which were expected to produce valuable products for export as well as new church members.

Under the leadership of Serra and his successors, the Franciscans labored fifty-three years to build a chain of twenty-one missions stretched along the California coast from San Diego to beyond San Francisco. Thousands of Indians became Catholics and worked for the missions.

Historian Herbert E. Bolton has explained that Spain did not have enough people to settle the land it claimed in the New World, so it chose to settle American natives instead. According to Bolton, "Such an ideal called not only for the subjugation and control of the natives, but their civilization as well. To bring this end about, the rulers of Spain made use of the religious and humanitarian zeal of the missionaries, choosing them to be to the Indians not only preachers but also teachers and disciplinarians."[4]

Serra was an ideal choice to carry out this policy. As courageous as he was devout, he covered 24,000 miles on his missionary travels. Strong in his faith that his Lord would provide, he once began a journey of 900 miles supplied with only a loaf of bread and a piece of cheese.

In 1770, when Serra founded his second mission at Carmel on Monterey Bay (the first was at San Diego), he celebrated mass on the same spot where priests who had traveled with Captain Vizcaíno had held their religious service almost 170 years earlier. Serra described his exultation over this triumph for both his God and his country.

"Then all of us went over to a large cross . . . stretched out on the ground. We all assisted in raising it and I blessed it, chanting the prayers of benediction. Then we planted it in the ground and all of us venerated it with all the tenderness of our hearts. With holy water I blessed those fields. Thus with the standard of the King of Heaven raised, the standards of our Catholic monarch were also set up, the one ceremony being accompanied by shouts of 'Long live the Faith!' and the other by 'Long live the King!'"[5]

The missions dominated religion, business, and education in California for seventy years. In 1829, a Boston businessman named Alfred Robinson visited several missions to buy animal hides for his company to ship east. Robinson's record of his trip included a description of San Gabriel Mission, a prosperous commercial and religious center with a population of about 1,200.

"As we approached," Robinson wrote, "the chapel bells tolled the hour for prayer. Hundreds of Indians were kneeling upon the ground and, as the tolling ceased, they slowly rose to retire, and a merry peal announced the coming of the Sabbath.

"The director of San Gabriel was Father Jose Sanches. . . . Possessing a kind, generous and lively disposition, he had acquired in consequence a multitude of friends who

A sketch of the Mission of San Gabriel, near Los Angeles

constantly flocked around him, whilst through his liberality the needy wanderer, of whatever nation or creed, found a home and protection. . . ."

Mission property included, besides the main compound, two ranches, a mill, fruit trees, gardens, and a lake. Robinson continued:

"There are several extensive gardens attached to this Mission, where may be found oranges, citrons, limes, apples, pears, peaches, pomegranates, figs and grapes in abundance. From the latter they make yearly from four to six hundred barrels of wine and two hundred of brandy, the sale of which produces an income of more than twelve thousand dollars. The storehouses and the granaries are kept well supplied and the corridor in the square is usually heaped up with piles of hides and tallow. Besides the resources of the vineyard, the Mission derives considerable revenue from the sale of grain and the weekly slaughter of cattle produces a sufficient sum for clothing and supporting the Indians. . . ."[6]

The success of the missions came at major cost to the Native Americans. An 1826 visitor to the same mission, Harrison G. Rogers, noted that they "are kept in great fear; for the least offense they are corrected; they are compleat slaves in every sense of the word."[7]

The power of the missions began to decline in the 1830s. Spain was no longer strong enough to maintain its foreign empire and stopped funding its faraway outposts. There was a revolution in Mexico, and, especially after the 1848 gold strike, settlers from the United States surged into California, soon overwhelming the influence of the Spanish Americans and their church.

Despite their brief history, the missions had an immense impact. The Franciscans had made converts and established the Catholic religion and Spanish language in California. They had taught many American Indians to read and write. They had taught thousands more how to plant and tend crops, weave cloth, and raise livestock. Before Father Serra began his work, natives were living the same simple way their ancestors had lived hundreds of years before. Before the missions, there had been not one horse or one steer in all of California. Sixty-five years later, mission Indians herded more than 60,000 horses and almost 400,000 cattle. With the missions, a new civilization came to California.

THE BOOK OF HEAVEN

While Eusebio Francisco Kino and Junípero Serra were busy in the Southwest, the British agents of the Hudson's Bay Company were at work in the North. The men who ran the company that eventually ruled the wilderness from mid-Canada to the Pacific Coast were in business to make money by trading in furs and other wilderness products. Their king and country reminded them, however, that they also had an obligation to their God.

When England's King Charles II granted a charter to the Hudson's Bay Company in 1670, his Colonial Office advised the New World traders: "You are to consider how the Indians and slaves may be best instructed in and united to the Christian religion; it being both for the honour of the Crown and of the Protestant religion itself, that all persons within any of our territories, though ever so remote, should be taught the knowledge of God and be made acquainted with the mysteries of salvation."[1]

But the practical company men still put business

King Charles II

before religion. They wanted trading posts in the wilderness, not churches.

Nevertheless, the Hudson's Bay Company in a curious and roundabout way fostered not only the ministers of its own Church of England but also other Protestant and Catholic missionaries who brought religion, education, and eventually permanent settlers to the Far West.

An unlikely instrument of change was an Indian boy known as Spokan Garry.

Garry, born in 1811, was the eldest son of Illim-Spokanee, chief of the peaceful and prosperous Spokane

Indians, the "Children of the Sun" who lived near the eastern border of what is now the state of Washington. Garry was fourteen years old when the Hudson's Bay Company turned his life upside down by taking him 1,000 miles away from his home and his people.

Sir George Simpson governed the company's far-flung operations west of the Rocky Mountains, including a trading post in the Spokanes' country. In 1825 Simpson wrote to Alexander Ross, the man in charge of the Spokane House outpost, that he wanted "two Indian boys of about eight years of age of the Spokane or Nez Perce tribe . . . for the purpose of being educated at the school."[2]

Simpson wanted to experiment. He speculated that the company would give young Indians a formal academic, religious, and practical education; when the boys were grown, they, in turn, could teach what they had learned to other members of their tribes. The special students would attend an established school located on the Red River, near Fort Garry (now Winnipeg), Canada, operated by the Church Missionary Society of the Church of England. The Reverend David Jones, the Anglican minister who ran the mission, was also chaplain to the Hudson's Bay employees and their families at Fort Garry.

Simpson's request for boys shocked the Indians. Give up their children, possibly never to see them again? It seemed unthinkable. And yet, after deep reflection and long discussions, they decided that they must make the sacrifice. More and more whites were coming to live among them; the whites' God was powerful. Learning the whites' ways and religion could help the natives adapt to the changes they knew were coming.

The chief of the Spokanes and the chief of the nearby

Kootenais offered their sons to Simpson, who baptized the children and gave them the names of two Hudson's Bay Company managers. The Indian boys became Spokan Garry and Kootenai Pelly.

Before he placed his son's hand in the hand of the white man who would take him far away, Chief Illim-Spokanee expressed his sorrow and his hopes:

"You see, we have given you our children, not our servants, or our slaves, but our own. We have given you our hearts—our children are our hearts—but bring them back again to us before they become white men. We wish to see them once more Indians, and after that you can make them white men if you like. But let them not get sick or die. If

This photo of Spokan Garry was taken in his later years. He died on January 12, 1892.

they get sick, we shall be sick; if they die, we shall die. Take them, they are now yours."[3]

Garry and Pelly began a three-month journey into the unknown in the company of strangers. They had no one to talk to—not even each other, because the Spokanes and the Kootenais spoke different languages.

The boys stayed at Red River for four years. They learned to read and write and to speak English and French. They cut their long hair and dressed in white men's clothes.

At home, the Spokanes and Kootenais wandered over their bountiful land, moving with the seasons to gather fish, berries, and roots, hunt game, and raise the fast horses they loved. At Red River, the Indian boys learned to stay in one place, till the land, plant crops, and harvest them as the whites did. They also learned to take part in the services of the Anglican Church and to pray to the white people's God.

After four years of school, Garry and Pelly returned to their tribes for a visit. They came home as devout Christians and dedicated teachers; each carried two gifts from their Red River instructors, an Anglican Book of Common Prayer and a King James Version of the Bible that the Indians would call the "book of heaven." The boys, who had grown into young men, were as eager to deliver their message of a new God as their Indian brothers and sisters were to hear it.

In a report to his Church Missionary Society in London, the Reverend Mr. Jones wrote from Red River: "The Indians on the Upper part of the Columbia paid utmost attention to the information conveyed to them through the boys . . . and readily received whatever instruction or doctrines they thought proper to inculcate . . . and ever since they assemble every Sunday to keep the Sabbath in the ways the boys directed."[4]

From Simpson's point of view, his education experiment was a success. When Garry and Pelly went east again to Red River in 1830, they took with them five more Indian boys from four tribes to be trained at the mission school. Pelly never saw his Kootenai family or his home again; he died in 1831 at Red River from injuries suffered earlier in a fall from a horse. Garry then traveled west once more to bring the sad news to his friend's family and Kootenai tribe.

This time Garry remained with his people, the Spokanes. He established a school that drew up to 100 students at a time, and he conducted church services every Sunday.

His daughter Nellie remembered: "Garry read the Bible to the Indians. I have read Garry's Bible. My father taught me how to pray; taught me a morning and an evening prayer; taught me my first religion."[5]

An Indian called Curley Jim said that Garry "told us of a God above. Showed us a book, the Bible, from which he read to us. He said to us, if we were good, that then when we died, we would go up above and see God."[6]

From Garry, the Spokanes and interested visitors from other tribes learned the Christian Ten Commandments and a Christian blessing to say before meals. He also tried to teach them English and how to grow garden vegetables and farm crops.

Garry and the other native boys schooled at Red River spread their influence throughout the Northwest. Garry became the most widely known of the group and worked the longest and the hardest to pass on to others what he had learned.

Travelers, including other missionaries, who visited the Oregon country over the next twenty years, wrote of their surprise at meeting peace-loving natives who seemed to know so much about the forms of Christian worship. According to their reports, many Indians would not work on Sundays but dressed in their best clothes and gathered in churchlike meetings. They held morning and evening services, knelt for prayers, listened attentively to their leader's sermonlike speeches, and punctuated the proceedings with low moans that sounded something like "amens."

In a description of his trip to the Northwest in 1835, the Protestant missionary the Reverend Samuel Parker said the Indians had learned these religious practices from Garry and the other Red River students. "What they did was to teach their tribesmen to observe Sunday and to worship God in the ways described," Parker said.[7]

In 1831, members of the Nez Perce people, neighbors of the Spokanes and Kootenais, began an almost legendary quest for more religion. They sent their representatives on a 2,000-mile journey to Saint Louis to seek help from their old friend the explorer William Clark, supervisor of Indian affairs in the Missouri River country. Clark and Meriwether Lewis had visited the Nez Perce twenty-five years before, when the explorers had blazed their trail across the West to the Pacific Ocean.

The four Indians who survived the perilous trip to Saint Louis asked Clark to send "black robes" (ministers) and the "book of heaven" to their people.

Historians have offered several possible explanations for the Nez Perce people's desire for more of the whites' religion. One strong theory is that Catholic Iroquois Indians from the Northeast, who had stayed with the Nez

Perce after traveling west with French-Canadian fur traders, urged the tribe to find priests.

But there also is substantial evidence to support the belief that Spokan Garry was the primary force that sent the natives on their amazing journey.

In 1839 the Reverend A. B. Smith, a Protestant missionary working among the Nez Perce, wrote: "About ten years ago a young Spokan who goes by the name of Spokan Garry who had been at the Red River School, returned. My teacher, the Lawyer [a Nez Perce chief], saw him and learned from him respecting the Sabbath and some other things which [Garry] had heard at the school. This was the first that he [Lawyer] had heard about the Sabbath and it was called by them, Halahpawit. He returned and communicated what he had heard to his people. Soon after which six individuals set out for the States, in search, as he says of Christian teachers."[8]

The Hudson's Bay Company used its power to oppose permanent American settlements in the Northwest, especially north of the Columbia River. It wanted the Oregon country to remain under British control and continue to supply wilderness products for trade.

Nevertheless, it may be that Spokan Garry—the boy the company chose to educate and raise as a white man—inspired the Nez Perce to ask for the missionaries who, in turn, helped bring the settlers who would claim the Northwest for the United States.

3

THE MISSIONARIES

The religious community in the East found the Indians' request for missionaries irresistible.

William Clark relayed the request to Catholic and Protestant church officials. William Walker, a Wyandot Indian chief who later became provisional governor of Kansas, wrote an eloquent letter to a friend in New York, G. P. Disoway. He told of meeting "three chiefs from the Flat Head nation" in Clark's office and of the Indians' sincere desire to bring more knowledge of the whites' Great Spirit to their people.

Walker's letter was reprinted widely in church journals, along with a ringing appeal from Disoway, who was a founder of the Methodist Episcopal Church Missionary Society.

"There are immense plains, mountains and forests in those regions whence they came, the abodes of numerous savage tribes. But no apostle of Christ has yet had the courage to penetrate into their moral darkness," Disoway thundered.

"Adventurous and daring fur traders only have visited these regions. . . . May we not indulge the hope that the day is not far distant when the missionaries will penetrate into these wilds where the Sabbath bell has never yet tolled since the world began! . . . Not a thought of converting or civilizing them ever enters the mind of the sordid, demoralizing hunters and fur traders. . . . Let the Church awake from her slumbers and go forth in her strength to the salvation of these wandering sons of the native forest!"[1]

For the next twenty years the church was wide awake and missionaries were going forth to the Northwest. Catholics and Protestants came by land and sea. They came to teach as well as preach.

The Methodists arrived there first. In 1834 they sent Jason Lee to answer the Nez Perces' call. Lee, whose six-foot, three-inch frame was as sturdy as his faith, was in charge of a group that included his nephew Daniel, also an ordained minister, and three assistants, including a schoolteacher named Cyrus Shephard. The pious churchmen traveled in strange company. Their companions and guides were rough fur traders led by Nathaniel Wyeth, who had explored the Oregon country on an earlier trip and now hoped to make his fortune there.

Lee had intended to work among the Nez Perce in the Rocky Mountains. Instead, he took the advice of John McLoughlin, the helpful Hudson's Bay Company factor (agent) at Fort Vancouver near the Pacific Ocean, and settled in the Willamette Valley, south of the Columbia River and about seventy-five miles from the fort.

A few months after the Methodist party arrived, Shephard reported in a letter to church officials back east that "Brother Lee preached at this fort on Sabbath, 28th

September, which were the first two sermons ever preached in this region, west of the Rocky Mountains."

While the rest of the Lee group worked at building a mission, Shephard stayed at Fort Vancouver to teach school. His students, he wrote to his superiors, were mostly "half-breed children . . . who, but for the advantage of instruction derived from their connection with the school, would be in little, if any better situation than the natives themselves. Some of them have made very laudable improvement in reading, spelling, writing, English grammar; and a few of the most advanced are now studying, in addition to these, geography and mathematics."[2]

Over the next few years, more Methodist men and women braved the long voyage from New England— around the tip of South America and up the West Coast—to help Lee expand the influence of their church. By 1840, there were sixty-five Methodists operating missions north, south and east of Fort Vancouver.

The Presbyterians and Congregationalists were close behind. In 1835 Dr. Marcus Whitman and the Reverend Samuel Parker set out for the Oregon country to survey the possibilities. Partway there, Whitman returned to the East to enlist helpers and arrange for supplies while Parker continued west to look for suitable mission sites.

By 1836 Whitman was ready. He had acquired the church authorities' blessing and support for his venture. He also had a new wife, the beautiful Narcissa, and had enlisted another couple, the Reverend Henry Harmon Spalding and his bride, Eliza. The Spaldings, while willing, were less than ideal helpmates. Eliza was not physically strong but answered her husband's concerns with a firm "I like the command just as it stands, 'Go ye into all the world'—and no exceptions for poor health."[3] Henry was bad-tempered, some say because he had once asked Narcissa to marry him and had been refused. But determination overcame their differences and the foursome came west. Narcissa and Eliza occupy a special niche in history: they opened the Oregon Trail to white women by riding horseback, on sidesaddles, across the plains and over the mountains to the Columbia River.

The Whitmans established their famous, and doomed, mission among the Cayuse Indians at Waiilatpu, near the present city of Walla Walla in southeast Washington. The Spaldings settled farther east with the Nez Perce Indians at Lapwai in what is now Idaho.

Soon they were joined by four more couples, who traveled west together in 1838. Mary and Elkanah Walker, Myra and Cushing Eells, Mary and William Gray, and Sarah and Asa Smith had their Christian religion and courage in common but did not get on well together. The strain of riding horseback for thirty miles a day and sharing two crowded tents at night probably magnified their differences, and they had frequent arguments. The plain-speaking Mary Walker wrote in her diary: "We have a strange company of missionaries. Scarcely one who is not intolerable on some account."[4]

The missionaries planned to establish permanent settlements and teach the Indians to live as they did. "No savage people, to my knowledge have ever become Christianized upon the wing," said the Reverend Mr. Spalding.[5] "We must use the plough as well as the Bible, if we would do anything to benefit the Indians. They must be settled before they can be enlightened," agreed the Reverend Mr. Walker.[6]

The Walkers and Eellses built their mission among the Spokanes, a short distance from the place where Spokan Garry had set up his first school ten years earlier. Garry was polite to the newcomers but not overly pleased with their attempts to teach his people a religion different from his own Anglican faith. He did, however, work with Walker to produce a written translation of the Ten Commandments in the Indians' language.

The Smiths settled at Kamiah, east of the Spaldings at Lapwai, and the Grays went to Yakima River country, west of the Whitmans.

Hard on the heels of the Protestants came Catholic priests, who penetrated the wilderness to establish lonely outposts among the inland and coastal Indian peoples. François Blanchet and Modeste Demers came from Red River, Canada. Pierre-Jean De Smet, born in Belgium, was working with Indians in Council Bluffs, Iowa, when he met the Nez Perce delegation on its way to Saint Louis and was inspired to push west a few years later.

Father De Smet was a traveling man. From his head-quarters at St. Mary's Mission in Montana, he covered some 50,000 miles to bring his religion to Native Americans throughout the Northwest. He became so well known that his mailing address was a simple "Saint Mary's, Rocky Mountains."

Father De Smet also made sixteen trips to Europe. On one of them he recruited six determined Catholic nuns, sisters of Notre Dame, who endured a nightmarish seven-month sea voyage from Belgium to the Columbia River to build a school in the forests of Oregon. The Sisters were truly in a New World, but they were equal to the challenge.

Sister Mary Loyola wrote to their home convent in

Father De Smet traveled throughout the Northwest.

Belgium: "Like Mary and Joseph we have come to what we may call Egypt. They had Jesus with them, strove to render one another happy, and so we find our joy in our simple community life, we too, live on what Providence sends."[7]

Of them all, the most unlikely laborer for the Christian Lord in what his church viewed as the fields of Northwest heathen was the Reverend Herbert Beaver. The Hudson's Bay Company sent Beaver to Fort Vancouver in 1836 as "chaplain and missionary for the education and religious instruction of the Indians."[8]

Beaver, thirty-six years old, was a proper English gentleman. He attended Oxford University. He was an ordained Anglican priest who gloried in the formal ceremonies of worship practiced by his tradition-laden Church of England. An acquaintance described him as "a man below medium height, light brown hair, grey eyes, light complexion, a feminine voice with large pretentions to oratory, a poor delivery and no energy."[9]

As unsuited as he was for the job, the Reverend Mr. Beaver found himself in the wilds of America, uneasy about living and working among what he considered the uncouth inhabitants of the Northwest.

In Oregon, Beaver was as out of place as a crumpet among clams. He complained almost from the first moment he and his wife, known as "haughty Jane," stepped off the ship at Fort Vancouver.

The Reverend Mr. Beaver was shocked at the behavior of company workers, who lived with their wives without being formally married. He refused to perform burial services because the dead had not been baptized and were "absolute heathens." And he refused to serve the Indians whom he had been sent to help.

Beaver quarreled constantly with the post's factor, John McLoughlin, a man famous for his hospitality and his ability to govern the company's Oregon empire with dictatorial firmness. Beaver refused to follow McLoughlin's orders and told his Hudson's Bay bosses that the governor was a disgrace to the company.

McLoughlin allowed Beaver to supervise the fort's school but warned him not to give the students religious instruction because most were Roman Catholics, as McLoughlin was. Beaver argued that since many of the children were orphans, there was no one to object if they were taught to be Anglicans instead of Catholics.

The righteous Beaver did not want any interference, even from the popular Narcissa Whitman and Eliza Spalding, who tried to help at the school while visiting the fort. Beaver wrote them a stiff note:

"Mr. Beaver presents his compliments to Mrs. Whitman and Mrs. Spalding, and, as he is aware that various customs prevail in different countries, begs respectfully to inform them, that it is unusual in England for any person to take part, without his permission and request, in the parochial duties of the minister. . . .

"He would, therefore, hope that, after this explanation, the Ladies . . . will refrain from teaching, in any respect, the children of the School at Vancouver, over which he has charge. . . ."[10]

Furthermore, complained Beaver to London, "When the missionaries went from the Fort the other day, I was shocked . . . at hearing that the scholars . . . had been paraded on the River Beach, and sung there an hymn. Sacred music should only be used on solemn occasions, but it is made here a common entertainment of an evening, without the slightest religious feeling."[11]

Beaver warned against any encouragement of American missionaries because "when they, or their followers, become numerous, the interests of the Company will be undermined."[12]

Bad as his reports were, Beaver told his superiors that they could have been much worse. "I might have affirmed, in general, that no Englishman, no gentleman, no Christian, no Clergyman, no married couple could possibly remain here, without having their feelings daily outraged by every species of conduct offensive to their former habits."[13]

This chart, called the Protestant Ladder, was designed by Henry Spalding and his wife to explain Christianity to the Indians.

The Reverend Herbert Beaver was unhappy about being sent to teach the Indians.

Beaver suffered Oregon for only two years and left it no better than he found it.

But the unhappy Mr. Beaver was right about one thing: when the American missionaries became numerous, they did undermine the interests of the Hudson's Bay

Company. They encouraged the settlers and farming that pushed out the traders, though they did not succeed in persuading many Indians to adopt their faith formally and permanently. When Myra Eells sorrowfully summed up her mission's labors among the Spokane, she expressed the disappointment shared by many of her co-workers throughout the Northwest: "We have been here nine years and have not yet been permitted to hear the cries of one penitent or the songs of one redeemed soul."[14]

The Eellses and the Walkers had made a promising beginning: eighty students came to their new school in 1839. But the Indians soon lost interest, and the missionaries were uncomfortable among the natives. After visiting the Spokane mission in 1841, Father De Smet noted that the preacher families cultivated a farm just large enough to supply themselves. "It appears that they are fearful that, should they cultivate more, they might have too frequent visits from the savages. They even try to prevent their encampment in their immediate neighborhood, and therefore they see and converse but seldom with the heathens, whom they have come so far to seek."[15]

The Whitmans and the Spaldings did only slightly better. They counted twenty-two converts in eleven years. The Whitmans spent more and more of their time helping the ever-increasing numbers of Oregon Trail pioneers passing through. Narcissa was too proud to make Indian friends, and an observer said that Marcus was so busy he "could never stop to parley." The Spaldings got along well with the Nez Perce at Lapwai and made a good beginning, but by 1846 the Indians had mostly lost interest in copying the whites' ways. Lapwai's once-thriving school had failed, and Spalding said that there was "not the least probability that there will ever be one here again."[16]

A missionary teaching the Indians

It is small wonder that the few missionaries failed in their attempt to bring sudden change to the lifestyle and culture of thousands of Indians. As the Reverend Mr. Walker concluded, "It is as hard and unnatural for [the natives] to lead a settled life as it would be for a New England farmer to change and lead a wandering life."[17]

Then, on November 29, 1847, the Cayuse Indians

murdered Marcus, Narcissa, and seven other whites at the Whitmans' Waiilatpu mission. Five other injured whites died within a week, and forty-six women and children were taken captive. The pressure within the tribe that exploded into tragedy had been building for some years. The Cayuse Indians had become more and more worried about the large number of white settlers who were coming to occupy their land. Three years earlier a white had killed a young chief of the Walla Wallas, who was visiting California, and angry Indians had talked of taking Whitman's life in exchange. The most immediate causes of the massacre were epidemics of scarlet fever and measles which, despite Dr. Whitman's best efforts, killed half the Cayuse tribe. The Indians focused their fears and anger on the whites at the Whitman mission and blamed them for their troubles. Other missions closed soon after the murders, until only three Catholic outposts remained in the Northwest.

The men and women who came west for God did not realize their high hopes, but they had an immense influence in ways beyond religion. They served as advance scouts and then as welcoming committees for the hundreds of thousands who came after them to settle the West.

The missionaries spread knowledge about the West by taking in curious visitors, who carried home tales of a beautiful and fertile land. They offered shelter and sympathy to weary Oregon Trail travelers and, by their example, proved that families could make homes in the wilderness. The mission schools and colleges, founded by Catholics and Protestants, provided a base for the Northwest's future system of education.

The missionaries also pushed the U.S. government to

make the Oregon country part of the United States. On trips back east, Jason Lee and Marcus Whitman, among others, fed the dreams of future pioneers with their writings and lectures and the publicity that surrounded their appearances.

Whitman helped guide a long wagon train that carried some 1,000 settlers west in 1843, the beginning of the Great Migration over the Oregon Trail. During the next forty years, almost 300,000 pioneers would follow.

THE TEACHERS

To the pioneers, the West had land, enough for everyone with the daring to go after it and the determination to work it. And it had treasure, waiting to be picked up. The 1848 discovery of gold at Sutter's Mill, near Sacramento, worked like a magnet, pulling eager fortune hunters from the East, the rest of the West, and around the world to California.

As other gold strikes were made, prospectors pursued their dreams of quick riches into the Utah Territory, the Southwest, and the Northwest. Merchants, gamblers, and others who could make money in mining towns followed them. Many discouraged miners who did not strike it rich settled down as farmers and ranchers. The end of the Civil War in 1865 and the completion of the first transcontinental railroad in 1869 brought ex-soldiers, railroad workers, and other settlers to the West.

The wilderness was filling up with people, including families with children. The newcomers wanted schools; as early as 1849 the first Oregon Territory legislature set aside land to support public education. They also needed teachers.

The pioneers found teachers, trained or untrained, wherever they could, paid them very little, and asked them to work in living rooms, shacks, half-finished buildings, primitive one-room schoolhouses, and occasionally, under the open sky. It was common for a "schoolmarm" to live with the family of a student, often in crowded, uncomfortable quarters; a typical teacher complained she had to move in with a different family every two weeks and walk three to six miles to school and back in all weather.

In the early years, school supplies, including books, were hard to come by. In the Northwest, cedar planks were used as blackboards. ABC primers and other books were often homemade, bound with scraps of gingham. Some teachers used newspapers as reading texts. Students wrote on slates that could be erased and used again instead of on paper. One pioneer remembered that the only pencils at his school were made of lead bullets sharpened to a point.

During the last quarter of the nineteenth century, wages for teaching averaged about $12 a month, although one unhappy young woman said she got $2 a week, paid in the spring after the county collected its dog tax. Another, who ran a school in her home, took in 50¢ per week per student. Sometimes families paid in goods rather than money. After completing one term, a young teacher recalled wryly: "The parents were kind in their expressions of appreciation for my services. I collected twenty-three dozen eggs in material award."[1]

Whatever teachers earned, it was little enough to compensate for the difficult and even dangerous conditions under which many of them worked. An incident in Virginia City, Nevada, provides an extreme example.

46

Students in a public school of the mid-1800s did not have individual desks.

The town, home of the fabulous Comstock Lode, was certainly the richest and possibly the wildest mining camp in the West. During the twenty years after the 1859 strike there, the Comstock produced over $300 million in gold and silver. The miners played as hard as they worked. Gunplay was commonplace.

Attempts to establish a school failed when the pupils

This 1867 photo shows one of the mines that was operated as part of the Comstock Lode.

frightened away teachers by shooting at them. But students met their match in mild-appearing Professor Harry Flotz, a failed miner who favored Virginia City-style methods of discipline.

Flotz faced his class armed with three revolvers and a large knife. When a student talked during the geography lesson, Flotz aimed a gun at the culprit and issued a quiet but convincing order: "Don't do that again. I never give a second warning."[2]

Other teaching posts were less alarming. But in most places in the still-raw West a teacher's qualifications included a little book learning and a lot of courage and determination. Fainthearts need not apply.

Angie Brigham met all the requirements. She traveled with her family by wagon train over the Santa Fe Trail and arrived in Prescott, Arizona Territory, in 1875, when she was twenty-one years old. She had graduated from college with honors and was a fine singer and musician.

Angie could teach anywhere. One of her primitive schoolhouses was a former chicken coop, with walls of cottonwood poles and a roof of brush. Wind blew through the walls. Rain leaked through the roof. Pesky, biting mites left by the chickens crawled over the children.

If conditions got too bad, Angie moved her class to the bottom of a dry, fifteen-foot-deep well in the school yard.

A photo of the school where gun-toting Professor Harry Flotz taught

There at least they could escape the wind and the bugs. One day when the county school superintendent came to call, he searched for the young teacher and her students and nearly fell into the well before he found them. Angie looked up and calmly invited her employer to come down and hear her pupils recite their lessons.

When Angie died in 1909, the local newspaper noted that: "When it was known in Prescott that she was to sing in one of the local churches on any particular Sunday evening, the gambling games of the town would all close up and the managers and well-known characters of these public resorts as well as the populace generally, would march to the house of worship in squads for the sole purpose of listening to her singing and playing."[3]

It was also said that after listening to the pretty girl with the sweet voice, the gamblers left generous contributions in the church collection plate before returning to their poker games.

Agnes Cleaveland was equally resourceful. When she was sixteen years old, her New Mexico Territory rancher neighbors recruited her to teach because no one else was available. Her training consisted of two terms of school in Philadelphia. She recalled: "So I answered the call of duty and a school was set up in a log cabin on the Ole Zaccarison place. It entailed a daily fourteen-mile horseback trip for teacher. . . .

"The student body of twelve ranged from little Early Wheeler and Owen Dean, both under six, to Gus Wheeler, who topped me in age by a few months and in stature by almost a foot. Gus furnished the school with its major problem in discipline. Naturally he didn't want to do what the younger ones did and the younger ones did want to do what Gus did, notably spend recess in target practice with Gus's forty-five, which he wore to school and was with difficulty persuaded to lay aside in the schoolroom.

"'I never go without a gun,' Gus told me. 'No tellin when I might need it. . . . I needed it at the other school I went to. When the teacher tried to make me do something I didn't want to, I shot up through the roof and scairt the liver out of him. He quit teachin' before very long.'

"'You won't scare the liver out of me by shooting through the roof,' I promised him. He looked at me with a calculating eye.

"'You can't make me do nuthin I don't want to,' he said.

"'Oh, can't I?' and I lunged at him. I struck him in the pit of the stomach. He crumpled with the impact and surprise of it.

"'That wasn't fair,' I told him when he had regained his breath, 'but you didn't play fair either. Suppose we call it quits.'

"'Quits it is,' he grinned sheepishly, looking around to reassure himself that none of the younger children had been witness to his downfall."[4]

Agnes's school year and her teaching career ended abruptly because "my pony was pawed to death before our horrified eyes by a vicious stallion who broke through the fence to attack him. . . ."[5]

Particularly in the early years, many frontier schools were informal and unregulated. The only requirements were children to attend and someone willing to teach.

In the 1870s, Mrs. Mary Mathews was a widow in a California mining town, taking care of herself and her son, Charlie. To make money, she started a school, did sewing,

It was not unusual for a frontier teacher to have thirty or forty students of varying ages.

and washed clothes for her neighbors. This is how she described her school and her busy days:

"Mrs. Calvin came in one day, and after hearing me instruct Charlie in his lesson, asked me why I would not start a select school. I said I would if I could get scholars enough.

"'Will twelve do?' said she.

"I said it would.

"'Well, just keep my baby for me, and I will get you some,' said Mrs. Calvin.

"She was gone about two hours and when she came

back she had twelve names. The children would commence on the following Monday.

"Monday came, and with it twelve as bright-looking children as you would wish to see. They were very smart, and learned very fast.

"In time my school numbered twenty. I now was able to lay up a little every week till I had $35 laid by. . . .

"I got up early every Monday morning, and got my clothes all washed and boiled and in the rinsing water; then commenced my school at nine. At noon I spent my leisure time sewing; and after school I did the same after I got my supper out of the way. I often sewed till twelve and one o'clock at night.

"Tuesday morning I had my clothes on the line by daylight and my breakfast ready.

"After breakfast my work was soon done up, and I sewed again till nine o'clock.

"At noon I starched all my clothes. After school I ironed as many of them as I could, and at night finished the rest of them. . . ."[6]

As communities grew, private schools, usually supported by churches, flourished, and public school districts were organized. Teachers were often recruited from the East.

Miss Mattie Hyde of Oshkosh, Wisconsin, came west to the new city of Spokane Falls, Washington Territory, in 1882. She was in her early twenties and just out of teachers' college when she was hired to teach the six upper grades in the boomtown's new, two-room school.

Miss Hyde had forty students, the youngest about twelve and the oldest twenty-two. Two of her star pupils did not have much time for homework; they spent their evenings dealing cards in the gambling houses. Yet another came with a note from one of the most feared tough guys in town, warning the teacher that anyone who messed with the boy would answer to his short-tempered protector.[7]

It is not surprising that after a brief teaching career, Mattie Hyde gave up her job to marry a shoe salesman.

One wonders what Hyde thought of another Spokane educator, Charles Albert Absolom, who was the headmaster and only teacher at the Rodney Morris Episcopal School for boys. Absolom was British, a graduate of Cambridge University in England, a cricket player, and a dandy dresser. At the annual school parade, he led his students down the street, twirling a walking stick and splendidly dressed in a top hat, long coat, white vest, gray trousers, spats and, as a finishing touch, bright yellow gloves.[8]

There were some homegrown teachers, too. Mary Robinson Gilkey, a pioneer teacher and Oregon native, told her story to a newspaper writer in 1922. It reads like a capsule history of the West.

Gilkey's mother and father met in 1844 when they traveled together on one of the earliest Oregon Trail wagon trains. Mary was born in 1846 in a log cabin on her parents' homestead near Dayton, Oregon Territory.

"One of the earliest recollections of my childhood," Gilkey recounted, "is of Father coming to the door of our log cabin riding a horse and leading a pack horse. This was in the spring of 1849. He kissed me good-bye, and Mother told me he was going away off, to be gone a long while to mine for gold in California. . . . Father came back after awhile from the California gold fields with less money than he had taken there."[9]

Gilkey's fondest memory is of her neighbor, Mrs. Odell, a schoolteacher from Maine.

"She influenced my life more than any other person. The first carpet I ever saw was in her home. The first potted plant I ever saw was at Mrs. Odell's house. The pioneer families owned but few books, and the first library I ever saw was at the home of Mrs. Odell. . . . I remember how astonished I was when I stayed at her house to dinner and she handed me a napkin. I did not know what it was. I had never seen one before and did not like to use it for fear I would get it spoiled.

"One evening as [Mrs. Odell] came home from school I saw she was carrying a plant she had dug up. I asked her what she was going to do with that wild flower. She said she was going to look in a book and see what its name was. I remember how profoundly astonished I was to think someone had written this plant's name in a book. . . . That was my first introduction to Botany. Next to my mother, I never loved anyone so much as Mrs. Odell."[10]

When Mary was thirteen years old, a school friend's brother asked her to marry him. "Remember . . . a great many of the girls in that day were married at 13. I told him I didn't care to get married—that I wanted to know something, that I wanted to come and go as I pleased and later I wanted to become a teacher. I told him Mrs. Odell was my ideal. . . ."[11]

Mary Robinson went to Lafayette Academy near her home, then to the Academy and Female Seminary in Portland, Oregon. In 1866 she graduated from Willamette University in Salem, where a daughter of the pioneer missionary Jason Lee was in charge of women students.

Mary Robinson knew exactly what she wanted to do with her life. As she explained, "It is not strange that in those days when there were so many more men than young women, I received a great many proposals, but I was wedded to my profession, teaching, and for 14 years I continued it. . . ."[12]

Leoti West was another wedded to teaching. She called herself an "old maid school ma'am," weighed 200 pounds and, in 1877, at the age of twenty-six, held a respectable but dull post as principal of the English Department at a business college in Dubuque, Iowa. But Leoti West was an adventurer who could not resist the call of the frontier. In 1878 she packed her bags and set off by train, boat, and stagecoach to accept the job of starting a Baptist school in the tiny town of Colfax in the southeast corner of the Washington Territory.

West, a lifelong teacher, remembered with pride that Colfax Academy was "the first high school of any description located in Eastern Washington. . . . Those who have lived their lives in the midst of a settled population where good schools are numerous, cannot begin to appreciate what Colfax College in its crude beginnings was to the young people of Washington at that period."[13]

The academy opened on September 11, 1878, in the still-unfinished Baptist Church building. There were seventeen pupils; by December the number had grown to fifty. But Leoti West was not one to sit and wait for students to walk in the door.

As she wrote later, "But something more than teaching was needful to build up a school. Visits to pioneer homes, face to face contact with the parents of those we would teach became a real necessity, and the summer vacation is the time when the Palouse hills must be scoured if we would have pupils for the next term.

"Comfortably seated upon the hurricane deck of an Indian pony, commonly called a cayuse, we are ready to begin the work . . . we find [the horse] in the main reliable, and with our two hundred pounds of avoirdupois upon his back he is not given to many lively antics. . . . "[14]

The "school ma'am's" first stop was at "the home of a good Baptist Deacon. . . . Some years prior to this time his good wife died, leaving him with eleven children. Later he met a widow, also with eleven children, and the two were married. One child was born to them, and now, with a family of twenty-three, they were a godsend to a struggling school in need of students."[15]

West rode on over the rolling Palouse hills, enjoying the scenery and the people, despite a few hardships. She stayed one night with another "good Baptist family."

"These people live in some style, in a palatial three-roomed house with real windows. Here we are successful in securing a promise of two pupils, and are fed on potatoes weighing from four to five pounds. We don't eat many, and have such an interview with bedbugs during the night as we hope never to experience again. We felt that we had, indeed, ridden into the valley of discomfort with a vengeance. Baptist bedbugs are no more agreeable companions than are those of other denominations."[16]

West summed up her recruiting trip, her experiences at Colfax Academy, and the rewards earned by dedicated teachers with characteristic good sense and good humor.

"We have been absent two weeks, have ridden two hundred miles and our entire expense for self and horse has been one dollar and twenty-five cents. Can a Methodist circuit rider present a better showing than this? Truly these good people are all friends to the old maid school ma'am.

"In the spring of '83 we sever our connection with the school; but never while we live can we forget the noble boys and girls who stood and still stand so loyally by their old teacher. We are ready from our experience to assert again and yet again that the compensation of the true secular teacher, like that of the true preacher of Christ's Gospel—the two are close akin—is not measured in dollars and cents, but in the consciousness of faithful service freely given and in the love and esteem of those she has tried to help."[17]

5

THE PREACHERS

A pioneer once explained why religion appealed to the local roughnecks. They miss their mothers, he said, and church reminds them of their mothers.

The western miners, cowboys, and settlers were a long way from their old homes, friends, and families. They were lonely, and the women in particular hungered for the social as well as the spiritual comfort of their religion.

Lucy Ide, with her husband and three children, traveled west by wagon train from Wisconsin in 1878. At the beginning of the diary she kept during the trip, she described the sadness of leaving her friends.

"Commenced my journey to the far far west. The hardest of all is bidding farewell to my near & dear friends, many of whom I fear I have seen for the last time on earth. We stopped to Mrs. Baileys to bid her good bye she gave me some butter and a cheese God bless her. . . . Here we part with Mr. & Mrs. Fisher also Mr. Claflin comes out to bid us good bye and I sincerely hope it is all the old friends I shall have to part with. It is almost more than I can bear. May the Lord spare them to meet again but who can tell. . . ."[1]

Elen Hevly, a young wife and mother homesteading near Puget Sound in 1880, wrote to her sister back in South Dakota: "When I think of father and mother and the many others in Dakota, I just hope, as I live here, that I will have an opportunity to see them, if the good Lord is willing to let me live for a while.

"I hear you had a meeting [church service] at Christmas time and my main wish was I could have been there, too. . . . We have not had a meeting since we came here. You can well imagine, Hanna, that it is quite lonesome to live in such a place where God's word is forgotten. I never thought, while I was in Dakota, that I would miss this as much as I do, but we have to be patient and hope that times will be better."[2]

Early missionaries had come to the West to teach their Christian religion to the native Indians. Later, preachers came to cultivate the faith of the white Christian settlers who had arrived before them. Pioneer families wanted churches as much as, or even more than, they wanted schools. As they had throughout the history of the West, preaching and teaching often went together.

In many western towns one building served double duty as church and school. And it was not unusual for the minister's wife to be pressed into service as schoolmarm. The Reverend David Blaine was the first permanent minister in Seattle, and his wife, Catherine, was the first schoolteacher. Seattle was founded in 1851. The Blaines arrived just two years later, traveling by ship and by land across the Isthmus of Panama from their home in Seneca Falls,

New York. The Methodist minister did not waste any time getting started on his Lord's work. In a letter home he wrote:

"We reached Alki [across the bay from Seattle] on Saturday, November 26. . . . We were very kindly received and hospitably entertained at a Mr. Russell's, the only white family in the place, which contains 8 or 9 houses and a sawmill. The houses are used as stores and homes for bachelors. . . . In the evening after the sermon, a young man took his hat, of his own accord, and passed it around among the auditors, of whom I should think there were 30. He turned out the contents on the table and I scraped them off and put them in my pocket. When we counted the money it amounted to $12.50."[3]

It was a good beginning. Within two years the minister had raised enough money to build Seattle's first church. His wife, no less energetic, operated her school Tuesdays through Saturdays. No classes on Monday, she insisted, because Monday was washday.

Some preachers, like Blaine, were sent west by church organizations. Others came on their own. In 1886 a newspaper reported: "A cowboy revivalist called 'Lampas Jake' is stirring the boys up down in New Mexico and Arizona. He preaches in frontier saloons and dance houses, and enforces attention with a six-shooter. Although illiterate he is said to be sincere and in dead earnest."[4]

Perhaps Lampas Jake was inspired by another "dead earnest" preacher named Endicott Peabody, who had arrived a few years earlier to bring religion to Tombstone, Arizona Territory, sometimes known as Helldorado.

Peabody was twenty-five years old when he arrived in Tombstone in 1882. He had come from the Episcopal

Catherine Blaine established the first schoolhouse in Seattle in the early 1850s.

Theological School in Boston to take a six-month job preaching in the roaring mining town whose most famous resident was the legendary gunfighter and lawman Wyatt Earp.

The young man seemed an unlikely choice for the job. He came from a prominent Massachusetts family, had grown up among educated, cultured people, and was a graduate of Cambridge University in England. He did not appear to be the type to mingle with Tombstone's miners and gamblers. But Peabody was an instant success in

Arizona, partly because he got along well with all kinds of people and partly because he was an outstanding athlete.

The *Epitaph*, a Tombstone newspaper, reported: "Well, we've got a parson who doesn't flirt with girls, who doesn't drink behind the door and when it comes to baseball, he's a daisy."

Peabody organized and starred on the first baseball team in Tombstone. He was also one of the few men brave enough to work as an umpire. Arizona gamblers bet big money on games between town teams, and rowdy fans came loaded with short tempers and long guns. The miners loved baseball, and because they worked six days a week, they played on Sundays. Peabody agreed to umpire on one condition: players must attend church before the game.

A typical Arizona gambling saloon around 1900

Westerners admired physical courage and strength. The popularity of the young minister from Boston grew when they discovered he was as talented in the ring as he was on the baseball diamond. As Tombstone's top boxer, Peabody never lost a bout and became a hero to the miners when he defeated their champion, a man much bigger than the hard-punching preacher.

Peabody needed cash to build a church. So he went where the money was—the saloons and gambling halls, where he filled his hat with contributions. On one occasion, the story goes, the preacher approached a group of poker players who had more than $1,000 on the table. Peabody quickly collected $150 from each player.

Peabody built his church, the first Protestant church in Arizona.

Peabody went back to Boston after six months and, a few years later, founded Groton, an exclusive New England prep school for boys. But Tombstone never forgot its favorite minister. When he visited Arizona forty years later, Peabody's old friends came from all over the state to hear him speak.[5]

The West also had some preachers who wore army uniforms. After the Civil War ended in 1865, the army established forts throughout the West. Soldiers fought the Indians, built telegraph lines, and protected settlers, supply trains, stage lines, army paymasters (who carried large amounts of money), and railroad construction workers. Military chaplains were stationed with the troops to provide moral guidance and also to organize schools for children and soldiers who lived at the forts. Chaplains were officers who began their service with the rank of captain. Besides his religious and educational duties, a chaplain

The Reverend Endicott Peabody built the first Episcopal church in Tombstone, Arizona, in 1882. Sixty-two years later, on March 4, 1944, Reverend Peabody conducted services at the White House commemorating President Roosevelt's eleventh year in office.

also often managed his post's library, garden, kitchen, and general store.

Allen Allensworth served as chaplain with the 24th Infantry from 1886 to 1906, the only black officer assigned to the all-black regiment. At that time the army put all of its black soldiers, who made up 10 percent of the troops, into two cavalry and two infantry regiments led by white officers. During Allensworth's years with the 24th, the much praised regiment served throughout the Southwest, north to Montana and west to California. During the Spanish-American War it fought overseas in Cuba and the Philippines.

Allensworth was born a slave in Kentucky in 1842 but learned to read and write while playing with his master's children. He fled to freedom just after the Civil War began, and first volunteered to help nurse wounded Union soldiers. Then he joined the United States Navy, working his way up to the highest rank open to an enlisted man.

After the war ended, Allensworth went to work as a government teacher, became a Baptist minister, and graduated from college. When Allensworth decided he wanted to be chaplain of the 24th Infantry he wrote to President Grover Cleveland, telling the president that the position would be "in keeping with my calling and I feel that I can be of service in securing good discipline and gentlemanly conduct among the soldiers."

Allensworth won his appointment and had a distinguished army career, retiring with the rank of lieutenant colonel. He believed that learning was the key to the advancement of blacks and won praise for his work as an educator. He trained soldiers to teach in the post schools and wrote one of the first military manuals used for troop education throughout the army.

While the regiment was stationed in Salt Lake City, the local newspaper said that "the rank and file of the Twenty-fourth has seemed to act all the time as though each soldier was upon his honor not to cause a reproach

Lieutenant Colonel Allen Allensworth

upon the uniform he wears or the flag above him. There seems to be a double influence for good always with the regiment. One is that of pride which the soldier feels in his profession, and the other is the counsels, influences and example of Chaplain Allensworth."[6]

The most familiar religious figures in the developing West probably were the traveling preachers often called circuit riders. The riders covered great distances by buggy or horseback in all weathers to bring the comfort of the church to remote settlements and homesteads. Members of their congregations, scattered over hundreds of miles, waited for the preacher to arrive to celebrate their marriages, baptize their babies, and comfort them in their sorrow for lost loved ones.

Some of the circuit riders were well educated, but many were self-taught and self-chosen. William Wesley Van Orsdel, known throughout Montana as Brother Van, was a circuit-riding Methodist preacher for almost fifty years. He was twenty-four years old when he arrived by steamboat at Fort Benton, Montana Territory, in 1872.

A circuit rider was a preacher who traveled to places that had no churches.

Brother Van had no money, no job, no training, no education. He wasn't even an official minister, just a young man from Pennsylvania who was convinced it was God's will that he come west to save souls.

Brother Van's faith never wavered. For forty-seven years he traveled, holding revival meetings, preaching, and making friends. He is credited with founding more than a hundred churches, a university, six hospitals, and a children's home. Montana had Indian reservations, mining towns, ranches, dirt-poor homesteads, and a very few cities scattered over vast open spaces. The traveling preacher visited them all and was welcome everywhere.

Along with his many virtues, Brother Van had at least one small flaw. He was a trifle vain. An admirer told about observing the preacher one night when Brother Van stayed with his family:

"Since our 16 by 16 shack with adobe addition was crowded with a family of seven plus other transient boarders, it was necessary that I sleep with Brother Van. I well remember him kneeling at the bedside for prayer. His balding head caused him more embarrassment than was evident to the outside world. He always carried horehound candy in his vest pocket which he would dampen to touch up his hair. The candy, when wetted, became sticky, and he would swirl his hair around in an attempt to make it cover as much as possible of the bald pate, using the candy to stick it into place."[7]

An entry from Brother Van's journal, dated August 1882, gives the flavor of the life of a circuit rider.

"I made my first trip into the Judith Basin on horseback. Stayed all night at the Severance ranch, about six miles south of Judith Gap, where the Barrows road house was then. Great excitement prevailed because the Indians had run off some horses the night before. At this time I met Mr. Morrison, proprietor of the new town of Philbrook, about 30 miles north. He gave the new hotel building, which was almost completed, for us to hold services in the following sabbath. There was a large turnout, the settlers coming from many miles in several directions to attend the first preaching service ever held in Fergus County. The small daughter of Clarence Barnes was baptized, and this was the first baptism ever performed in that area.

"From there I went to Pig Eye Basin, where I met C. C. David and family, about 18 miles from Philbrook. I met Sister David some distance from the house. She was afoot, looking for the horses, which it was soon learned the Indians had stolen. From there I crossed the Belt Mountains and spent the next sabbath at Barker, where I held services that morning and evening. From there the next day I went to Neihart where I held a service that evening. At that time, no ladies had ever been in that town. There were about 20 men in the mining camp, all of whom were at the service."[8]

It was said of Brother Van that there was not a dog in Montana that would not wag his tail when he saw him coming. Any traveling preacher would recognize that as high praise.[9]

6

THE CHILDREN

In 1909 teacher Alice Orwiler mailed a picture postcard addressed to "Papa Orwiler, Plaza, Wash." at the family farm, located about seventy-five miles north of the small town of Pomeroy, where she worked. On one side of the postcard was a picture of Alice, nineteen years old, with her twelve students. The group was posed in front of its one-room schoolhouse, squinting into the sun. One sturdy blond youngster was taller than her teacher, and the smallest girl was holding the teacher's hand.

On the other side of the card, Alice had written: "Hello Dad: Here 'is me' and my kids. Aren't they a bright-looking bunch?"[1]

The picture could have been taken almost anywhere in the West around the turn of the century. Plain, one-room buildings housing young teachers with their students of all ages dotted the rural areas. There were no buses to transport pupils long distances to a large, central building. A school had to be located near the children's homes so that students could reach it on foot or on horseback.

A horse-drawn wagon often served as a "school bus" around 1900.

Nelia Binford Fleming, a daughter of a southeast Washington Territory homesteader, described her 1880s school as "a single room, unceiled, unpainted, almost unfurnished. The stove sat in the middle of the room, and the stove pipe ran out the end of the room, right over the heads of any pupil who sat under its path. . . . There were benches of rough boards, along the walls on two sides of the room. Nails were driven into the wall above the benches, and we hung our wraps on these nails and put our lunches on the long bench. The father of each family of children attending school made desks enough to supply his brood, and took them to the school house. Some were large, some were small, some smooth, some rough, some well made, some very sketchily put together. Each child supplied his own books, and took to school and studied whatever sort of book the family happened to possess. So classes were almost impossible to organize. . . .

"Big boys who seemed men to me . . . came to school. One day, one of these big fellows wanted to show off, so climbed up to the joists under the roof, and sat there and swung his legs, laughing, nor would he come down until he so desired.

"One year there were sixty children, big and little, of all ages and grades, huddled into that one room, sitting on those hard seats, sometimes crowded three in a seat, for lack of room. . . ."[2]

School terms were short. Nelia Fleming recalls: "We had only three months of school in a year, so ran wild the rest of the time, except that Mother would settle us all down for a little study each day. "[3]

Despite the obstacles, children did learn. Like Alice Orwiler, many pioneer teachers were fond and proud of their eager students, and often the admiration was mutual.

Milton Shatraw, son of a Montana rancher, remembered his first teacher as his first love. "One night I sat with my family and the two ranch hands around the kitchen table. All eyes were on the living room door. At last it was pushed slowly open and there she stood—smiling, blue eyes, golden hair, fashionable clothes—the new teacher. I was six, and instantly and hopelessly in love. . . .

"Most of our teachers came from some mysterious place called 'back East.' They stayed at our ranch and lived with us as a member of the family, helping my mother during their spare time and sharing all our activities, even our affection. At least this particular girl did. Perhaps it was she who sparked me with the love of books and interest in learning which I have had ever since she took me by the hand and led me across the prairie to school."[4]

The Montanan's schoolhouse was built of "undressed logs, notched at the corners and chinked with mortar . . . the floorboards failed to reach quite to the wall, leaving a gap of several inches. . . . In winter the snow drifted up under this gap and a snowbank lined the walls, sometimes for days, until the wood fire in the sheet-iron stove would gain the upper hand and melt it away. . . . Since we kept on all our outdoor clothing except mittens and caps during severe cold spells, the scent of scorched leather and overheated wool pervaded the school. . . . In spring and fall, a trip to the privy was something of a field excursion and enjoyed to the limit of the teacher's patience. But in winter, nothing but dire necessity drove us to those snowbound outhouses."[5]

As grown-ups, pioneers who wrote about their school days recalled mostly happy times. But while many school days in the old West were good, there were some bad ones, just as there are today.

Marianne Hunsaker Edwards D'Arcy remembered how lonely she was when she was sent to live at a boarding school. Marianne traveled to the Oregon Territory in 1846 when she was four years old. She was a young child when

A wood stove was a fixture in most one-room schoolhouses.

her parents took her and her two sisters to the school in Oregon City operated by the Catholic nuns that Father Pierre-Jean De Smet had brought from Belgium. The child was terrified, sure that her mother and father had left her forever.

"I cried myself to sleep every night. One of the older girls said most of the girls at the school were orphans. I wanted to know what that was and she said, 'Their folks are dead, or gone to California to the gold fields. I guess your folks have decided to abandon you and have given you to the sisters.' I was so panic-stricken and homesick that I nearly died, for I thought I should never see my mother again. . . . [Later] one of my sisters decided to be a nun. Mother decided that for a good Baptist to become a nun would never do, so they took us out of that school."[6]

The federal government set up separate schools for Indians, so that most children in the public schools were white. Those who were not had to struggle to secure their rightful place in the education system.

During the 1850s thousands of Chinese began arriving in California, hoping to strike it rich in "Gum Shan, the Golden Mountain." American churches sent missionaries to San Francisco to preach Christianity to these newest immigrants. As part of their work, the missions held English classes. For many years after the first mission opened in 1853, the churches were the only places that Chinatown residents could go to learn English. San Francisco's Chinese children were not allowed to attend public school with whites until the 1920s.[7]

In Seattle, Mattie Harris told what it was like for her and her brother as schoolchildren about 1900. "We were the only Black at Warren Avenue School. . . . They were pretty snooty. They seemed to accept my brother. . . . He was maybe a different type, maybe he was more pushy, but anyhow they accepted him. He'd fight for his way, and when you start fighting the way opens. [I had] plenty of problems. Some of the teachers weren't too nice. If it was a group picked out to do something, you weren't in that group."[8]

A primary school for Chinese in early San Francisco

At about the same time, a Chinese girl was having a similar experience in Nogales, Arizona.

"We used to have problems . . . when we were going to school," Marian Lim recalled. "The Mexican kids used to tease us because we were Chinese. There were some Mexican boys in our neighborhood who would always take my brother and beat him up. My brother Frank, who was smaller and younger, would cry. One day I told them that if they didn't stop bothering him I was going to go after them. So they didn't believe me. One day they teased my brother so much I went after them and I beat one up

77

something terrible. . . . After that they never bothered Frank anymore."[9]

Mary Paik Lee, who came to California with her family in 1906, was one of only three dozen Korean children in the entire Pacific Coast region at that time. Mary's father had been a church minister in Korea, but in California he worked first in the fruit orchards, then as a tenant farmer, and finally selling fruit.

"In those days," Mary Lee explained, "Orientals and others were not allowed to live in town with the white people. The Japanese, Chinese, Mexicans and Filipinos each had their own little settlement outside of town. . . .

"When I was ready to go to school, Father asked a friend who spoke a little English, Mr. Song, to take me. It was a very frightening experience. As we entered the schoolyard, several girls formed a ring around us, singing a song and dancing in a circle. When they stopped, each one came to me and hit me in the neck, hurting and frightening me. They ran away when a tall woman came towards us. Her bright yellow hair and big blue eyes looking down at me were a fearful sight; it was my first close look at such a person. When she addressed me, I answered in Korean, 'I don't understand you,' turned around, ran all the way home and hid. The next day when I went to school with my brother the girls did not dance around us; I guess the teacher must have told them not to do it. I learned later that the song they sang was:

> Ching Chong, Chinaman,
> Sitting on a wall,
> Along came a white man,
> Who chopped his head off.

"The last line was the signal for each girl to chop my head off by giving me a blow on the neck. That must have been the greeting they gave to all the Oriental kids the first day they came to our school."[10]

Kazuko Monica Sone, a Japanese American born in Seattle a few years later, enjoyed going to public school but disliked, at first, the much stricter Japanese school that her parents insisted she also attend in the late afternoons. As she explained in her autobiography, it was difficult to reconcile two cultures in one child.

"Gradually I yielded to my double dose of schooling. Nihon Gakko was so different from grammar school I found myself switching my personality back and forth daily like a chameleon. At Bailey Gatzert [public] School I was a jumping, screaming, roustabout Yankee, but at the stroke of three when the school bell rang and doors burst open everywhere, spewing out pupils like jelly beans from a broken bag, I suddenly became a modest, faltering, earnest little Japanese girl with a small, timid voice. . . .

"As far as I was concerned Nihon Gakko was a total loss. . . . Promptly at five-thirty every day, I shed Nihon Gakko and returned to an environment which was the only real one to me. Life was too urgent, too exciting, too colorful for me to be sitting quietly in the parlor and contemplating a spray of chrysanthemums in a bowl as a cousin of mine might be doing in Osaka."[11]

GROWING UP

Once established, education and religion, like the rest of the American West, grew up fast. In 1892, when settlers gathered to tell tales of their early days in the Pacific Northwest, the Reverend Myron Eells joked that some questioned his right to join the group because "I never crossed the plains as other pioneers did."[1]

True, Eells had never experienced the hardships of the Oregon Trail. However, he pointed out with some pride, "I think myself that I am one kind of a pioneer, at least—a pioneer baby."[2] Eells was born in 1843 at Tshimakain Mission, near the present city of Spokane, Washington. His parents, Cushing and Myra Eells, were part of the group of New England Protestant missionaries who came to the Oregon wilderness in 1838, two years after the Whitmans and the Spaldings had shown the way.

Myron Eells carried on the family tradition and became a minister who spent his life working with Puget Sound Indian peoples. But first he was one of those who brought the story of the opening of the West full circle: he was a westerner who went East, a place that to him was as unknown and dangerous as the West once had been to his parents.

Eells was graduated from Pacific University in Forest Grove, Oregon, with the class of 1866. Then, as he told the story: "President S. H. Marsh, D.D., of that university once said to me that I was born and brought up on this coast and had obtained my education here, and was a pretty good specimen of an Oregonian, and that what I still needed was to go east and become an American. In the summer of 1868 I determined to do so, having decided to study for the ministry. Rev. J. E. Walker, now of China, went with me—both green Oregonians—but we helped each other, and so probably kept out of some snaps in which we otherwise might have got caught. . . . Having never been in any place larger than Portland, then a place of less than 8,000 people, we naturally felt uneasy when our first jump was into San Francisco and our next into the little village of New York City."[3]

The two young men saw the sights in San Francisco, endured bad food and uncomfortable beds during a voyage down the coast, took a train across the Isthmus of Panama, and then another ship up the East Coast to New York, where they did not linger: "We determined to leave the city as soon as possible because we had heard so much about the pickpockets, and then return and see the sights after we had learned the ways of the world."[4]

Eells spent a lonely first year at school in New England. "At first I felt as much alone as a person could . . . for there was hardly more than one person there of whom I had ever heard, and I felt as if I were in water up to my

New York City in 1878

mouth, which was sometimes coming in, and only could get breath enough to live on, but I lived through it. The students, too, were about as much surprised to see a person who had come from Washington territory who knew anything, as if I had rained down."[5]

Eells spent his vacations traveling. Although often uneasy in new places, he avoided serious problems by following his father's advice: "Be cautious among strangers."

He also kept his goal in mind: "I tried . . . to get acquainted with my own country and become an American."[6]

Over the next fifty years, other westerners did the same.

By the 1920s some Spokane children were attending a two-story brick elementary school similar to schools found everywhere in the United States at that time. A former pupil remembers: "The students would line up in order of their classes and arrange themselves according to height to march silently to their classrooms, accompanied by a duet played by two young girls on an upstairs piano."[7]

The school stood not far from the place where, some 100 years before, Indians had come to a pole-and-rush shack to hear their teacher, Spokan Garry, share the lessons and the religion he had learned from the white men in far-away Red River.

Garry died in 1892. He lived long enough to see the wise man's prophecy, told to him as a boy by his father the chief, come true. The arrival of strangers bearing "leaves bound together in a bundle"—the preachers and teachers and other "strange people with a skin of a different color"—marked the end of one world in the West and the beginning of another.

SOURCE NOTES

THE PROPHECY

1. Thomas E. Jessett, *Chief Spokan Garry* (Minneapolis: T. S. Denison, 1960), 16–17.

1. FOR GOD AND SPAIN

1. W. Storrs Lee, ed., *California: A Literary Chronicle* (New York: Funk and Wagnalls, 1968), 19.

2. George Pierre Castile, ed., introduction to *The Indians of Puget Sound, the Notebooks of Myron Eells* (Seattle: University of Washington Press, 1985), xvii.

3. Lee, *California: A Literary Chronicle*, 25.

4. Paul C. Johnson, ed., *The California Missions* (Menlo Park, Cal.: Lane Book, 1964), 32.

5. Don De Nevi and Noel Moholy, *Junípero Serra* (New York: Harper and Row, 1985), 101.

6. Lee, *California: A Literary Chronicle*, 91–94.

7. Harrison Clifford Dale, *The Explorations of William H.*

Ashley and Jedidiah Smith, 1822–29 (Lincoln: University of Nebraska Press, 1991), 202.

2. THE BOOK OF HEAVEN

1. Peter C. Newman, *Company of Adventurers* (Ontario, Canada: Penguin, 1985), 89.

2. Jessett, *Chief Spokan Garry*, 21.

3. Ibid., 24.

4. Ibid., 35.

5. Talkington, *Heroes and Heroic Deeds of the Pacific Northwest* (Caldwell, Idaho: Caxton, 1929), 272.

6. Jessett, *Chief Spokan Garry*, 42.

7. Ibid., 70.

8. Ibid., 36.

3. THE MISSIONARIES

1. W. Storrs Lee, ed., *Washington State: A Literary Chronicle* (New York: Funk and Wagnalls, 1969), 139.

2. Clark C. Spence, *The American West: A Source Book* (New York: Thomas Y. Crowell, 1969), 87.

3. Cecil Dryden, *Dryden's History of Washington* (Portland, Ore.: Binford and Mort, 1968), 93.

4. Nancy Wilson Ross, *Westward the Women* (New York: Knopf, 1944), 61.

5. D. W. Meinig, *The Great Columbia Plain* (Seattle: University of Washington Press, 1968), 123.

6. Ibid., 25.

7. Ross, *Westward the Women*, 90.

8. Thomas E. Jessett, ed., *Reports and Letters of Herbert Beaver, 1836–1838* (Portland, Ore.: Champoeg Press, 1959), xiii.

9. Ibid., xii.

10. Ibid., 11.

11. Ibid., 22.

12. Ibid.

13. Ibid., 19.

14. Castile, *The Indians of Puget Sound, the Notebooks of Myron Eells*, xvii.

15. Dryden, *Dryden's History of Washington*, 136.

16. Meinig, *The Great Columbia Plain*, 141.

17. Dryden, *Dryden's History of Washington*, 137.

4. THE TEACHERS

1. Agnes Morley Cleaveland, *No Life for a Lady* (Lincoln: University of Nebraska Press, 1969), 126.

2. Irving Stone, *Men to Match My Mountains* (Garden City, New York: Doubleday, 1956), 240.

3. Obituary in *Prescott Journal Miner,* January 25, 1909.

4. Cleaveland, *No Life for a Lady*, 123.

5. Ibid., 125.

6. Christiane Fischer, ed., *Let Them Speak for Themselves: Women in the American West, 1849–1900* (Hamden, Conn.: Archon Books, 1977), 182–184.

7. Lucille F. Fargo, *Spokane Story* (Minneapolis: Northwestern Press, 1957), 131–135.

8. Ibid.

9. Fred Lockley, *Conversations with Pioneer Women.* Compiled and edited by Michael Helm. (Eugene, Ore.: Rainy Day Press, 1981), 177.

10. Ibid., 178.

11. Ibid., 181.

12. Ibid.

13. Leoti L. West, *A Chapter from the Life of a Pioneer Teacher* (Fairfield, Wash., Ye Galleon Press, 1986), 13.

14. Ibid., 14.

15. Ibid.

16. Ibid., 16.

17. Ibid., 18.

5. THE PREACHERS

1. Kenneth L. Holmes, ed., *Covered Wagon Women*, vol. 10 (Spokane: Arthur H. Clark, 1991), 61.

2. Elen Hevly to Hanna Haugan, February 24, 1880, in personal library of Nancy Hevly, Seattle.

3. Roberta Frye Watt, *Four Wagons West* (Portland, Ore.: Binford and Mort, 1931), 122.

4. Spence, *The American West: A Source Book*, 412.

5. Marshall Trimble, *In Old Arizona* (Phoenix: Golden West, 1895), 74.

6. John Phillip Langellier, "Chaplain Allen Allensworth and the 24th Infantry 1886–1906," *The Smoke Signal* (Tucson Corral of the Westerners, Fall 1980), 200.

7. Robert W. Lind, *Brother Van, Montana Circuit Rider* (Helena, Mont.: Falcon Press, 1992), 205.

8. Ibid., 149–150.

9. Ibid., ix.

6. THE CHILDREN

1. Alice Orwiler postcard to her father, Pomeroy, Wash., 1909, in personal library of Nancy Hevly, Seattle.

2. Nelia Binford Fleming, *Sketches of Early High Prairie* (Portland, Ore.: Binford and Mort, [1950?]), 12–29.

3. Ibid., 12.

4. Milton E. Shatraw, "School Days," *American West,*

magazine of the Western History Association, 3 (spring 1966): 68.

5. Ibid., 69.

6. Lockley, *Conversations with Pioneer Women*, 287.

7. Thomas W. Chinn, *Bridging the Pacific* (San Francisco: Chinese History Society of America, 1980), 1.

8. Mattie Harris, in Esther Mumford, *Seattle's Black Victorians 1852–1901* (Seattle: Ananse Press, 1980), 140–141.

9. Evelyn Hu-DeHart, Lawrence Fong, and Heather Hatcher, "The Chinese Experience in Arizona and Northern Mexico," reprinted from the *Journal of Arizona History,* 1980 (Tucson: Arizona Historical Society), 19.

10. Mary Paik Lee, "A Korean/Californian Girlhood," *California History,* magazine of the California Historical Society (March 1988): 42.

11. Monica Sone, *Nisei Daughter* (Seattle: University of Washington Press, 1979), 22, 28.

7. GROWING UP

1. Robert A. Bennett, ed., *A Small World of Our Own* (Walla Walla, Wash.: Pioneer Press, 1985), 351.

2. Ibid.

3. Ibid., 355.

4. Ibid., 357.

5. Ibid., 358.

6. Ibid., 359.

7. Shirley Frese Woods, *Whitman's Quarterly* 15 (spring 1993): 7.

FURTHER READING

BOOKS

Aaseng, Nathan. *From Rags to Riches*. Minneapolis: Lerner, 1990.

Alter, Judith. *Growing Up in the Old West*. Chicago: Watts, 1991.

————. *Women of the Old West*. New York: Watts, 1989.

Bakeless, John, ed. *The Journals of Lewis and Clark*. New York: Penguin, 1964.

Bennett, Robert Allen. *We'll All Go Home in the Spring*. Walla Walla, Wash.: Pioneer Press, 1984.

Binns, Archie. *Peter Skene Ogden: Fur Trader*. Portland, Ore.: Binford and Mort, 1967.

Blumberg, Rhoda. *The Great American Gold Rush*. New York: Macmillan, 1989.

Brown, Dee. *Gentle Tamers: Women in the Old Wild West*. Lincoln: University of Nebraska Press, 1968.

————. *Hear That Lonesome Whistle Blow: Railroads in the West*. New York: Holt, 1977.

Carter, Harvey L. *Dear Old Kit*. Norman: University of Oklahoma Press, 1968.

Clappe, Louise (Dame Shirley). *The Shirley Letters: From the*

California Mines, 1850–1852. Edited by Carl I. Wheat. New York: Knopf, 1961.

Clemens, Samuel Langhorne. *Roughing It.* New York: Holt, Rinehart and Winston, 1965.

De Nevi, Don, and Noel Moholy. *Junípero Serra.* New York: Harper and Row, 1985.

Erickson, Paul. *Daily Life in a Covered Wagon.* Washington, D.C.: Preservation Press, 1994.

Fischer, Christiane, ed. *Let Them Speak for Themselves: Women in the American West, 1849–1900.* Hamden, Conn.: Archon, 1977.

Fisher, Leonard Everett. *The Oregon Trail.* New York: Holiday, 1990.

Harte, Bret. *The Luck of Roaring Camp.* Providence, Rhode Island: Jamestown, 1976.

Hoobler, Dorothy, and Thomas Hoobler. *Treasure in the Stream: The Story of a Gold Rush Girl.* Morristown, New Jersey: Silver Burdett, 1991.

Jessett, Thomas E. *Chief Spokan Garry.* Minneapolis: T. S. Denison, 1960.

Johnson, Paul C., ed. *The California Missions.* Menlo Park, Cal.: Lane Book, 1964.

Katz, William. *The Black West.* Seattle: Open Hand, 1987.

Lapp, Rudolph. *Blacks in Gold Rush California.* New Haven: Yale University Press, 1977.

Lasky, Kathryn. *Beyond the Divide.* New York: Dell, 1986.

Levy, Jo Ann. *They Saw the Elephant.* Hamden, Conn.: Archon, 1990.

Lewis, Oscar. *Sutter's Fort: Gateway to the Gold Fields.* New York: Knopf, 1976.

Luchetti, Cathy, and Carol Olwell. *Women of the West.* Berkeley: Antelope Island Press, 1982.

McNeer, May. *The California Gold Rush.* New York: Random House, 1987.

Meltzer, Milton. *The Chinese Americans: A History in Their Own Words*. New York: HarperCollins, 1980.

Morris, Juddi. *The Harvey Girls: The Women Who Civilized the West*. New York: Walker, 1994.

Moynihan, Ruth B., Susan Armitage, and Christiane Fischer Duchamp, eds. *So Much to Be Done: Women Settlers on the Mining and Ranching Frontier*. Lincoln: University of Nebraska Press, 1990.

Nabakov, Peter. *Native American Testimony: An Anthology of Indian and White Relations, First Encounter to Dispossession*. New York: HarperCollins, 1972.

Rappaport, Doreen, ed. *American Women: Their Lives in Their Words*. New York: HarperCollins, 1992.

Ray, Delia. *Gold, the Klondike Adventure*. New York: Lodestar, 1989.

Schlissel, Lillian. *Women's Diaries of the Westward Journey*. New York: Shocken, 1982.

Smith, Carter. *Bridging the Continent: A Sourcebook on the American West*. Brookfield, Conn.: Millbrook Press, 1992.

Steber, Rick. *Grandpa's Stories*. Prineville, Ore.: Bonanza, 1991.

Stewart, George R. *The Pioneers Go West*. New York: Random House, 1987.

Stratton, Joanna. *Pioneer Women*. New York: Simon and Schuster, 1982.

The Trailblazers. *The Old West*. New York: Time-Life Books, 1979.

Tunis, Edwin. *Frontier Living*. New York: HarperCollins, 1976.

Van Steenwyk, Elizabeth. *The California Gold Rush: West with the Forty-niners*. Chicago: Watts, 1991.

Watt, James W. *Journal of Mule Train Packing in Eastern Washington in the 1860s*. Fairfield, Wash.: Ye Galleon Press, 1978.

Weis, Norman D. *Helldorados, Ghosts and Camps of the Old Southwest*. Caldwell, Idaho: Caxton Printers, 1977.

Wilder, Laura Ingalls. *West from Home*. New York: HarperCollins, 1974.

92

Wilson, Elinor. *Jim Beckwourth: Black Mountain Man and War Chief of the Crows*. Norman: University of Oklahoma Press, 1972.

Young, Alida O. *Land of the Iron Dragon*. New York: Doubleday, 1978.

TAPES AND COMPUTER SOFTWARE

American West: Myth and Reality, Clear View, CD-ROM.

Dare, Bluff, or Die, Software Tool Works, CD-ROM, DOS.

Miner's Cave, MECC, Apple II.

Morrow, Honere. *On to Oregon!* Recorded Books, Inc., Prince Frederick, Md. Three cassettes.

Murphy's Minerals, MECC, Apple II.

Oregon Trail II, CD-ROM, Windows.

The Oregon Trail, MECC, Apple II, MS-DOS, 1990.

Santa Fe Trail (Educational Activities).

Steber, Rick. *Grandpa's Stories*. Bonanza. Cassette.

Wagons West, Focus Media, 485 South Broadway, Suite 12, Hicksville, New York, 11801.

INDEX